Conversations
with Jesus

Jordan Whittington

Contents

An Introduction to Conversations with Jesus

Purpose:
Welcome to Conversations with Jesus, a study of the personal interactions of Jesus. This book is intended to guide small group discussion, to help members to have a more thorough understanding of the character and teaching of Jesus, and to encourage real life application of the scriptures. Each lesson has scripture to read (printed in the book to encourage annotations) and questions related to the text. Each member of the group should have a copy of this book so they can read the scriptures and answer the questions each week before meeting. My hope is that this book is a helpful resource for you and your group as you seek to learn to live and love like Jesus.

Sections:
Read the Word:
Each lesson starts with the scripture for the week. Take time to read and understand the message, context, and purpose of the text. So, read it as many times as you need in order to understand what you are reading. Mark up the text with notes, highlights, or even questions you have about the reading.

Examine the Word: After you have read through the text, it is time to interact with it. In each lesson, you will be prompted to write your "One Big Thing" and "One Confusing Thing", "One Way I Must Respond" and finally to articulate who Jesus is to the individual studied on both a practical and a spiritual level. These prompts are intended to help you consider the big picture of what you read. What stands out? What doesn't make sense? How does this apply?

Next, you will be prompted to consider a few questions. These questions are intended to make you think critically about the text. Take time to think through thorough and complete answers to the questions. Allow time to really think through your answers even if you think of an answer immediately. Make sure you write down your responses as a way to help you think and so you remember your thoughts during discussion.

Notes: Each text will have footnotes and other related verses to consider. These notes are meant to help you understand the scripture better and make connections to other texts. The goal of the notes is to assist in personal study, not to be an answer key. As you study the text, the notes will give you further insight to the language, context, and concepts of the text. The related verses should help you see how the conversation studied relates to the rest of the Bible.

Discussion: When you come together as a group, read the text together and discuss the questions. The questions are not meant to give strict order to the discussion, but they are a great starting point. I encourage you to share what you have learned, but go to your discussion with the primary goal of learning from the other members of your group.

Special thanks to Asher Ardizzoni for his help in developing questions, creating footnotes, and preparing the document for print.

Special thanks to Aaron Macias for his vision, creativity, and willingness to create cover art for each of our bible studies.

The Messengers from John

LESSON 1

The Messengers from John

Matthew 11:1-6

[1]When Jesus had finished instructing his twelve disciples, he went on from there to teach and preach in their cities.

[2]Now when John[1] heard in prison[2] about the deeds of the Christ, he sent word by his disciples [3]and said to him, "Are you the one who is to come, or shall we look for another?[3]" [4]And Jesus answered them, "Go and tell John what you hear and see: [5]the blind[4] receive their sight and the lame walk, lepers are cleansed and the deaf hear, and the dead are raised up, and the poor have good news preached to them.[5] [6]And blessed is the one who is not offended[6] by me."

One Big Thing:

One Confusing Thing:

What is John really asking Jesus? What is causing these questions?

---

[1] John the Baptist is the cousin of Jesus. John has a miraculous birth that points to God's plan for his life. John is the forerunner of Jesus who is sent to prepare the people for the Lamb of God that was coming into the world.

[2] John is in prison because his teachings have shamed Herod for his improper relationship with his sister-in-law now wife (See Matthew 14:1-5).

[3] John's question is a question of Jesus' messiahship.

[4] Jesus demonstrates all of the miracles listed in verse 4-5 in Matthew 8-9 (Blomberg, *Matthew*, 185).

[5] Jesus is calling John to look beyond his current situation to see understand that Jesus is meeting the expectations of the messiah (Stein, *Luke*, 225).

[6] Offended can be translated as take offense, stumble, or even cause to sin (Blomberg, *Matthew*, 185).

Read the previous confessions of John regarding Jesus. Who does John understand Jesus to be in the following verses?

Luke 1:44   *John 1:26-30*

John 3:34-36   *Matthew 3:13-15*

Why doesn't Jesus come right out and say he is the Messiah/the Son of God?

What circumstances in your life or aspects of the Christian faith have caused you to doubt? How have you dealt with these doubts?

Is it wrong to doubt your faith?

What are the appropriate steps to take when you doubt your faith?

How do you feel you would be perceived if you expressed your doubts to your Christian friends?

One Way I Must Respond

Who is Jesus to John?

Scriptures to consider:
Isaiah 61:1
Matthew 8:23-27
Matthew 14:1-12

The Woman at the Well

LESSON 2

The Woman at the Well
John 4:1-26

Now when Jesus learned that the Pharisees had heard that Jesus was making and baptizing more disciples than John [2] (although Jesus himself did not baptize, but only his disciples), [3] he left Judea and departed again for Galilee. [4] And he had to pass through Samaria. [5] So he came to a town of Samaria called Sychar, near the field that Jacob had given to his son Joseph. [6] Jacob's well was there; so Jesus, wearied as he was from his journey, was sitting beside the well. It was about the sixth hour.

[7] A woman from Samaria came to draw water.[1] Jesus said to her, "Give me a drink." [8] (For his disciples had gone away into the city to buy food.) [9] The Samaritan woman said to him, "How is it that you, a Jew, ask for a drink from me, a woman of Samaria?" (For Jews have no dealings with Samaritans.[2]) [10] Jesus answered her, "If you knew the gift of God, and who it is that is saying to you, 'Give me a drink,' you would have asked him, and he would have given you living water." [11] The woman said to him, "Sir, you have nothing to draw water with, and the well is deep. Where do you get that living[3] water? [12] Are you greater than our father Jacob? He gave us the well and drank from it himself, as did his sons and his livestock." [13] Jesus said to her, "Everyone who drinks of this water will be thirsty again, [14] but whoever drinks of the water that I will give him will never be thirsty again. The water that I will give him will become in him a spring of water welling up to eternal life." [15] The woman said to him, "Sir, give me this water, so that I will not be thirsty or have to come here to draw water."

[16] Jesus said to her, "Go, call your husband,[4] and come here." [17] The woman answered him, "I have no husband." Jesus said to her, "You are right in saying, 'I have no husband'; [18] for you have had five husbands, and the one you now have is not your husband. What you have said is true." [19] The woman said to him, "Sir, I perceive that you are a prophet. [20] Our fathers worshiped on this mountain, but you say that in Jerusalem is the place where people ought to worship." [21] Jesus said to her, "Woman, believe me, the hour is coming when neither on this mountain nor in Jerusalem will you worship the Father. [22] You worship what you do not know; we worship what we know, for salvation is from the Jews. [23] But the hour is coming, and is now here, when the true worshipers will worship the Father in spirit and truth,[5] for the Father is seeking such people to worship him. [24] God is spirit, and those who worship him must worship in spirit and truth." [25] The woman said to him, "I know that Messiah is coming (he who is called Christ). When he comes, he will tell us all things." [26] Jesus said to her, "I who speak to you am[6] he."

---

[1] Culturally, it is the woman's responsibility to draw water. This duty was often completed in the early morning or evening to avoid the heat of the day.

[2] The Samaritans were a mixed breed of Jewish heritage and Assyrian invaders. The intermarrying and subsequent intermixing of other religions led to a hostile divide between the Jews and Samaritans.

[3] Living water was water which came from a spring or stream and is the most valued source of water. Living water was the only water used in religious purification (Burge, *John*, 143).

[4] "Jesus commonly drives to the individual's greatest sin, hopelessness, guilt, despair, or need" (Carson, *John*, 221). Jesus shows that he is willing to work through even our deepest shame.

[5] Jesus is revealing that worship is more a matter of the heart than location. Worship "in spirit and truth" is worship that is true, pure, and singularly focused on the one deserving praise not on following specified rules and regulations.

[6] "I am" is a reference back to the name of God used throughout the Old Testament. God is the "Great I Am of Israel". By Jesus using this phrase, he is connecting himself to God.

One Big Thing:

One Confusing Thing:

Who is Jesus to the woman at the well?

What is shocking about Jesus' decision to talk to this woman? Is there a modern-day example of this?

What is Jesus' intention in asking her to bring her husband?

What barriers did Jesus cross? What societal barriers exist around us?

Which are you most hesitant to cross?

What does Jesus mean in his offer of "Living Water"? How does that differ from what she hears?

What does it mean to worship in Spirit and in Truth?

Read verses 28-30 and 39-42. How is she transformed and what comes out of her transformation?

One Way I Must Respond

Who is Jesus to the Woman at the Well?

Scriptures to consider:
John 14:6
Romans 6:23
1 John 1:8-9
Psalm 22:27

The Centurion

LESSON 3

The Centurion
Matthew 8:5-13

[5] When he had entered Capernaum, a centurion[1] came forward to him, appealing to him, [6] "Lord, my servant is lying paralyzed at home, suffering terribly." [7] And he said to him, "I will come and heal him." [8] But the centurion replied, "Lord, I am not worthy[2] to have you come under my roof,[3] but only say the word, and my servant will be healed. [9] For I too am a man under authority, with soldiers under me. And I say to one, 'Go,' and he goes, and to another, 'Come,' and he comes, and to my servant, 'Do this,' and he does it." [10] When Jesus heard this, he marveled and said to those who followed him, "Truly, I tell you, with no one in Israel have I found such faith.[4] [11] I tell you, many will come from east and west[5] and recline at table with Abraham, Isaac, and Jacob in the kingdom of heaven, [12] while the sons of the kingdom will be thrown into the outer darkness. In that place there will be weeping and gnashing of teeth." [13] And to the centurion Jesus said, "Go; let it be done for you as you have believed." And the servant was healed at that very moment.

One Big Thing:

One Confusing Thing:

---

[1] A military commander in charge of roughly 100 troops. Centurions were the face of Roman occupation in Israel (Blomberg, *Matthew*, 100).
[2] This is the same phrase used by John the Baptist when discussing untying the sandals of Jesus.
[3] While communication between Jews and Gentiles was common, relationship was not. A Jew would not enter the house of a Gentile in order to remain ceremonially clean.
[4] Jesus consistently praises the faith of gentiles while scolding the lack of faith of the Pharisees and even his own disciples.
[5] Jesus is breaking down ethnic barriers held by the Jews. The kingdom of God will be full of Gentiles who will feast alongside the heroes of Israel. See Ephesians 3:6 for more.

How does the Centurion show his faith?

What is significant about the Centurion's initial appeal for healing?

Where do you turn first when problems arise? List actual examples.

How do you personally put limits on what Jesus can do? → reword

We believe that God can, will, and wants to work for your good and His glory. Which of these do you struggle to believe most?

Jesus speaks of the inclusion of Gentiles into the Kingdom of God. What are the consequences/what is the significance of this? (See footnotes for context)

Compare and contrast earthly authority to the authority of Jesus.

One Way I Must Respond

Who is Jesus to the Centurion?

Scriptures to consider:
Ephesians 3:6
Ephesians 3:20-21
Matthew 15:21-28

The Mother of
James and John

The Mother of James and John

Matthew 20:20-28

[20] Then the mother of the sons of Zebedee[1] came up to him with her sons, and kneeling before him she asked him for something.[2] [21] And he said to her, "What do you want?" She said to him, "Say that these two sons of mine are to sit, one at your right hand[3] and one at your left, in your kingdom." [22] Jesus answered, "You do not know what you are asking. Are you able to drink the cup[4] that I am to drink?" They said to him, "We are able." [23] He said to them, "You will drink my cup, but to sit at my right hand and at my left is not mine to grant,[5] but it is for those for whom it has been prepared by my Father." [24] And when the ten heard it, they were indignant at the two brothers. [25] But Jesus called them to him and said, "You know that the rulers of the Gentiles lord it over them, and their great ones exercise authority over them. [26] It shall not be so among you. But whoever would be great among you must be your servant, [27] and whoever would be first among you must be your slave, [28] even as the Son of Man came not to be served but to serve, and to give his life as a ransom[6] for many."

One Big Thing:

One Confusing Thing:

---

[1] The Sons of Zebedee are James and John two of Jesus' twelve disciples. These two have left everything (family, jobs, security) to follow Jesus. See Matthew 4:21-22.

[2] Matthew's account reveals that James and John have requested their mother to do what they were unwilling to do yet strongly desired (Blomberg, *Matthew*, 306).

[3] The right and the left hand were seats of power and prestige.

[4] The cup is commonly used in the Old Testament as a metaphor for suffering. James and John will experience similar fates as Jesus as James was beheaded and John was exiled (MacArthur, *The MacArthur Bible Commentary*, 1162).

[5] While Jesus has all authority, he lays this power aside as he humbles himself when he becomes man and dwells on this Earth. Following his resurrection, Jesus' authority will be reestablished (Blomberg, *Matthew*, 307).

[6] Ransom is the payment required to set free a slave (Blomberg, *Matthew*, 308). Jesus as our ransom is setting free those who are slaves to sin by his sacrifice on the cross.

Why did James' and John's mother ask for this instead of them?

What was the mother really asking for? What was at the heart of the request?

What point is Jesus conveying as he concludes the conversation?

Compare and contrast this passage with Matthew 20:29-34. How does the request of the mother differ from the requests described in vv. 29-34?

How do the earthly concepts of greatness and status differ from what Jesus describes?

Are there certain situations in which you feel you have earned or deserve status? Where are you tempted towards selfishness?

What are some practical ways to live out "The first shall be last and the last shall be first"?

How are you practicing serving rather than being served? How must you improve?

One Way I Must Respond

Who is Jesus to the mother of James and John?

Scriptures to Consider:
Matthew 20:16
Matthew 7:7-11
Mark 10:45
Isaiah 51:17

Nicodemus

LESSON 5

Nicodemus

John 3:1-21

Now there was a man of the Pharisees[1] named Nicodemus[2], a ruler of the Jews. [2] This man came to Jesus by night and said to him, "Rabbi, we know that you are a teacher come from God, for no one can do these signs that you do unless God is with him." [3] Jesus answered him, "Truly, truly, I say to you, unless one is born again[3] he cannot[4] see the kingdom of God." [4] Nicodemus said to him, "How can a man be born when he is old? Can he enter a second time into his mother's womb and be born?" [5] Jesus answered, "Truly, truly, I say to you, unless one is born of water and the Spirit,[5] he cannot enter the kingdom of God. [6] That which is born of the flesh is flesh, and that which is born of the Spirit is spirit. [7] Do not marvel that I said to you, 'You must be born again.' [8] The wind blows where it wishes, and you hear its sound, but you do not know where it comes from or where it goes. So it is with everyone who is born of the Spirit."

[9] Nicodemus said to him, "How can these things be?" [10] Jesus answered him, "Are you the teacher of Israel and yet you do not understand these things? [11] Truly, truly, I say to you, we speak of what we know, and bear witness to what we have seen, but you do not receive our testimony. [12] If I have told you earthly things and you do not believe, how can you believe if I tell you heavenly things? [13] No one has ascended into heaven except he who descended from heaven, the Son of Man. [14] And as Moses lifted up the serpent in the wilderness, so must the Son of Man be lifted up, [15] that whoever believes in him may have eternal life.[6]

[16] "For God so loved the world, that he gave his only Son, that whoever believes in him should not perish but have eternal life. [17] For God did not send his Son into the world to condemn the world, but in order that the world might be saved through him. [18] Whoever believes in him is not condemned, but whoever does not believe is condemned already, because he has not believed in the name of the only Son of God.

---

[1] The Pharisees are the respected religious leaders of the day who live in strict observance to God's law.

[2] Nicodemus is a distinguished teacher that is well-respected and trusted (Carson, *John*, 186).

[3] To be born again (literally, born from above) is to be born anew spiritually (MacArthur, *The MacArthur Bible Commentary*, 1357).

[4] Salvation is not a work we can accomplish but a gift we must accept. New birth comes only by the power and work of God through our faith.

[5] To be born of water and spirit carries the imagery of being cleansed and renewed by God (Carson, *John*, 195).

[6] Eternal life is the generous gift of God given to all who follow him. Eternal life is a saving from the punishment deserved due to sin as well as a never-ending residence in Heaven and relationship with God.

One Big Thing:

One Confusing Thing:

Why does Nicodemus visit Jesus?

Rewrite John 3:16-18 in your own words. What stands out to you most in these verses?

In what ways does each person of the Trinity show up in Jesus' conversation with Nicodemus? Purpose?

Is v18 too harsh?

What is required to see/enter the Kingdom of God? What is not mentioned?

Do you think there are people who claim to be Christians who haven't been born again? Are they saved?

What evidence can we look to that someone has been born again? (*Need help? Read Galatians 5:22-26*)

One Way I Must Respond

Who is Jesus to Nicodemus?

Scriptures to consider:
John 7:50-52
John 19:38-42
1 Peter 1:22-23

The Rich Ruler

LESSON 6

The Rich Ruler
Luke 18:18-25

[18] And a ruler[1] asked him, "Good Teacher, what must I do to inherit eternal life?" [19] And Jesus said to him, "Why do you call me good? No one is good except God alone. [20] You know the commandments: 'Do not commit adultery, Do not murder, Do not steal, Do not bear false witness, Honor your father and mother.'" [21] And he said, "All these I have kept from my youth." [22] When Jesus heard this, he said to him, "One thing you still lack. Sell[2] all that you have and distribute to the poor, and you will have treasure in heaven; and come, follow[3] me." [23] But when he heard these things, he became very sad, for he was extremely rich.[4] [24] Jesus, seeing that he had become sad, said, "How difficult it is for those who have wealth to enter the kingdom of God! [25] For it is easier for a camel[5] to go through the eye of a needle than for a rich person to enter the kingdom of God."

One Big Thing:

One Confusing Thing:

---

[1] This man is" presented as a religious leader whose moral and religious life was exemplary" (Stein, *Luke*, 456).

[2] For the rich ruler, "his wealth has become his means to personal identity, power, purpose and meaning in life. It has in a real sense become his god" (Wilkins, *Matthew*, 649). Jesus is requiring him to give up what he feels is his greatest security (Stein, *Luke*, 457).

[3] Follow me is the repeated call throughout Jesus' ministry for would be disciples to lay aside everything for his sake.

[4] Great wealth caused for an even greater sacrifice. Far too often, wealth is a hindrance to salvation (Stein, *Luke*, 458).

[5] Jesus is being purposefully hyperbolic (extreme) to reveal how seriously one must handle possessions.

How does the ruler view Jesus?

Before Meeting Jesus   *Walking away from Jesus*

If you were asked – "What must I do to inherit eternal life?" – how would you answer?

Compare and contrast your response to Jesus' response.

Why does Jesus demand the rich man to give away his possessions but the only requirement he made of the disciples was to simply "follow me" (Matthew 4:18-22)?

What should a Christian's relationship with wealth look like?

Why did the ruler walk away sad?

Is there something you are holding onto like the ruler was holding onto his wealth?

One Way I Must Respond

Who is Jesus to the Rich Ruler?

Scriptures to Consider:
Matthew 6:24
Matthew 10:37
Matthew 16:24
Acts 16:31

Zacchaeus

LESSON 7

Zacchaeus
Luke 19:1-10

He entered Jericho[1] and was passing through. [2] And behold, there was a man named Zacchaeus.[2] He was a chief tax collector[3] and was rich. [3] And he was seeking to see who Jesus was, but on account of the crowd he could not, because he was small in stature. [4] So he ran on ahead and climbed up into a sycamore tree[4] to see him, for he was about to pass that way. [5] And when Jesus came to the place, he looked up and said to him, "Zacchaeus, hurry and come down, for I must stay at your house[5] today." [6] So he hurried and came down and received him joyfully. [7] And when they saw it, they[6] all grumbled, "He has gone in to be the guest of a man who is a sinner." [8] And Zacchaeus stood and said to the Lord, "Behold, Lord, the half of my goods I give to the poor. And if I have defrauded anyone of anything, I restore it fourfold."[7] [9] And Jesus said to him, "Today salvation has come to this house, since he also is a son of Abraham.[8] [10] For the Son of Man came to seek and to save the lost."

One Big Thing:

One Confusing Thing:

---

[1] You may recall Jericho as the first city in Israel's conquest (Joshua 4) of the Promised Land under Joshua's leadership. Jericho is also the scene where a blind man is healed by Jesus (Luke 18:35-43).
[2] Literally meaning, "Righteous One" (Stein, *Luke*, 467).
[3] Tax collectors were despised by the Jewish people as they were a constant reminder of enemy occupation in their land. Tax collectors were often seen as traitors since they abandoned their heritage in order to gain personal wealth at the expense of their own countrymen.
[4] The sycamore tree had low but sturdy branches which allowed for easy climbing for Zacchaeus (MacArthur, *The MacArthur Bible Commentary*, 1318).
[5] To enter a home of a person is to be in relationship with this person. Jesus initiates this relationship rather than waits for it to happen.
[6] Both the religious leaders as well as the common townspeople were surprised and upset over Jesus' relationship with Zacchaeus (Ibid.).
[7] Old testament law required repayment of money plus 20 percent in interest. Zacchaeus chooses to repay and adds 300 percent interest. Gratitude, not greed, is at the heart of how he handles his money (Kistemaker, *The Conversations of Jesus*, 75).
[8] Sons of Abraham would be understood as chosen people of God.

What is Jesus' intention in visiting with Zacchaeus?

What is Zacchaeus' reputation in his town? What evidence backs up this view?

Zacchaeus spent his life pursuing money only to find it did not satisfy? What are you tempted to pursue hoping it will satisfy?

"For the Son of Man came to seek and save the lost." How does this apply to you? Is Zacchaeus saved by his actions? Why or why not?

Who, in our society, is most like Zacchaeus and the tax collectors?

How does the idea of repentance tie into Zacchaeus' story?

Besides the fact that he loves all people, why does Jesus choose people that others overlook?

One Way I Must Respond

Who is Jesus to Zacchaeus?

Scriptures to Consider:
Luke 5:29-32
Romans 5:6-10
2 Samuel 12:1-6

The Blind Beggar

LESSON 8

The Blind Beggar

Mark 10:46-52

[46] And they came to Jericho. And as he was leaving Jericho with his disciples and a great crowd, Bartimaeus, a blind beggar,[1] the son of Timaeus, was sitting by the roadside. [47] And when he heard that it was Jesus of Nazareth, he began to cry out and say, "Jesus, Son of David,[2] have mercy on me!" [48] And many rebuked him, telling him to be silent. But he cried out all the more, "Son of David, have mercy on me!"[3] [49] And Jesus stopped and said, "Call him." And they called the blind man, saying to him, "Take heart. Get up; he is calling you." [50] And throwing off his cloak,[4] he sprang up and came to Jesus. [51] And Jesus said to him, "What do you want me to do for you?" And the blind man said to him, "Rabbi,[5] let me recover my sight." [52] And Jesus said to him, "Go your way; your faith has made you well." And immediately he recovered his sight and followed[6] him on the way.

One Big Thing:

One Confusing Thing:

Explain the significance of the ways Bartimaeus addresses Jesus.
Son of David (see 2 Samuel 7:8-9, 12-16)

Rabbi

Lord (see Matthew 20:31,33 Luke 18:41)

---

[1] Beggars often congregated outside the city gate which acted as a funnel for people entering and exiting the city.

[2] Bartimaeus is using Old Testament language to refer to Jesus as he understands him to be the promised one of God from the line of David (For more, see 2 Samuel 7).

[3] The plea of have mercy on me is a plea to Jesus to act with the compassion of God towards him.

[4] Most likely, the cloak was Bartimaeus' collection plate. By throwing it aside, he is no longer dependent upon the charity of others but is fully believing Jesus can and will show him mercy.

[5] Lord, not Rabbi is used in Matthew (20:31,33) and Luke (18:41).

[6] Faith leads to following.

Why does Jesus ask him what he wants?

Why does the crowd try to quiet Bartimaeus? Who are you tempted to silence?

What role does persistence play in our faith? Have you ever been tempted to quit?

How have the works of God encouraged you to follow Jesus? (Mark 10:52)

What role does sight play in this story both literally and figuratively?

In what areas have you lost sight of Jesus or the Gospel?

Does Bartimaeus' request change throughout his conversation with Jesus?

How does the blind man respond to both the call of Jesus and the healing of Jesus?

What can we apply from his responses?

One Way I Must Respond

Who is Jesus to the blind beggar?

Scriptures to Consider:
Matthew 7:7-11
Luke 4:18-19
2 Samuel 7:8-9, 12-16

Peter

LESSON 9

Peter

John 13:36-38

[36] Simon Peter said to him, "Lord, where are you going?"[1] Jesus answered him, "Where I am going you cannot follow me now, but you will follow afterward." [37] Peter said to him, "Lord, why can I not follow you now? I will lay down my life for you." [38] Jesus answered, "Will you lay down your life for me? Truly, truly, I say to you, the rooster will not crow[2] till you have denied me three times.

John 18:15-18 *(Jesus has been arrested and is brought to the religious leaders)* [15] Simon Peter followed Jesus, and so did another disciple. Since that disciple was known to the high priest, he entered with Jesus into the courtyard of the high priest, [16] but Peter stood outside at the door. So the other disciple, who was known to the high priest, went out and spoke to the servant girl who kept watch at the door, and brought Peter in. [17] The servant girl at the door said to Peter, "You also are not one of this man's disciples, are you?" He said, "I am not."[3] [18] Now the servants and officers had made a charcoal fire, because it was cold, and they were standing and warming themselves. Peter also was with them, standing and warming himself.

John 18:25-27

[25] Now Simon Peter was standing and warming himself. So they said to him, "You also are not one of his disciples, are you?" He denied it and said, "I am not." [26] One of the servants of the high priest, a relative of the man whose ear Peter had cut off, asked, "Did I not see you in the garden with him?" [27] Peter again denied it, and at once a rooster crowed.

John 21:15-19 *(Following his resurrection, Jesus visits his disciples)* [15] When they had finished breakfast, Jesus said to Simon Peter, "Simon, son of John, do you love me more than these?" He said to him, "Yes, Lord; you know that I love you." He said to him, "Feed[4] my lambs." [16] He said to him a second time, "Simon, son of John, do you love me?" He said to him, "Yes, Lord; you know that I love you." He said to him, "Tend my sheep." [17] He said to him the third time, "Simon, son of John, do you love me?" Peter was grieved because he said to him the third[5] time, "Do you love me?" and he said to him, "Lord, you know everything; you know that I love you." Jesus said to him, "Feed my sheep. [18] Truly, truly, I say to you, when you were young, you used to dress yourself and walk wherever you wanted, but when you are old, you will stretch out your hands, and another will dress you and carry you where you do not want to go." [19] (This he said to show by what kind of death he was to glorify God.) And after saying this he said to him, "Follow[6] me."

---

[1] Throughout the gospels, Jesus prepares his disciples for the crucifixion that is to come. Though warned, this reality does not sink in for the disciples until after Jesus' resurrection.

[2] It was typical for roosters to crow at 12:30 a.m., 1:30 a.m., and 2:30 a.m., resulting in this time slot being called the "cockcrow" (Carson, *John*, 487).

[3] John quotes Jesus on numerous occasions using the phrase "I am". Not only does this allow Jesus to show his multi-faceted roles for his followers, but it also reveals Jesus' divine nature as God was known as "I am". Peter's statement, "I am not" is ripe with connections.

[4] To feed the sheep/lambs is a constant devotion to nourishing the flock (MacArthur, *The MacArthur Bible Commentary*, 1427).

[5] Jesus chooses to question and restore Peter three times. I understand this to act as a symbolic restoration of each denial.

[6] The same language used to call Peter is now used to commission him, "Follow me."

One Big Thing:

One Confusing Thing:

Why does Peter deny Jesus?

What would tempt you to deny?

What feelings must Peter have felt when the rooster crowed the final time?

What failures have caused you to feel similar shame?

Jesus initiates reconciliation with Peter. What does this fact reveal to us about our Savior and God?

Why does Jesus ask Peter "do you love me"?

Why does he ask the same question three times?

Take a moment to answer the same question: Do you love me?

Read Luke 5:3-11. Compare and contrast the original call of Peter with this final commissioning of Peter.

One Way I Must Respond:

Who is Jesus to Peter?

Scriptures to consider:
Mark 1:16-18
John 6:67-69
Acts 4:19-20
Acts 4:7-12

Pilate

LESSON 10

Pilate
John 18:28-19:20 (CSB)

[28] Then they led Jesus from the house of Caiaphas to the governor's headquarters. It was early morning. They themselves did not enter the governor's headquarters, so that they would not be defiled, but could eat the Passover. [29] So Pilate[1] went outside to them and said, "What accusation do you bring against this man?" [30] They answered him, "If this man were not doing evil, we would not have delivered him over to you." [31] Pilate said to them, "Take him yourselves and judge him by your own law." The Jews said to him, "It is not lawful[2] for us to put anyone to death." [32] This was to fulfill the word that Jesus had spoken to show by what kind of death he was going to die.

[33] So Pilate entered his headquarters again and called Jesus and said to him, "Are you the King of the Jews?" [34] Jesus answered, "Do you say this of your own accord, or did others say it to you about me?" [35] Pilate answered, "Am I a Jew? Your own nation and the chief priests have delivered you over to me. What have you done?" [36] Jesus answered, "My kingdom is not of this world. If my kingdom were of this world, my servants would have been fighting, that I might not be delivered over to the Jews. But my kingdom is not from the world." [37] Then Pilate said to him, "So you are a king?" Jesus answered, "You say that I am a king. For this purpose I was born and for this purpose I have come into the world—to bear witness to the truth. Everyone who is of the truth listens to my voice." [38] Pilate said to him, "What is truth?"

After he had said this, he went back outside to the Jews and told them, "I find no guilt in him. [39] But you have a custom that I should release one man for you at the Passover. So do you want me to release to you the King of the Jews?" [40] They cried out again, "Not this man, but Barabbas!" Now Barabbas was a robber.

19 Then Pilate took Jesus and flogged[3] him. [2] And the soldiers twisted together a crown of thorns and put it on his head and arrayed him in a purple robe. [3] They came up to him, saying, "Hail, King of the Jews!" and struck him with their hands. [4] Pilate went out again and said to them, "See, I am bringing him out to you that you may know that I find no guilt in him." [5] So Jesus came out, wearing the crown of thorns and the purple robe.[4] Pilate said to them, "Behold the man!" [6] When the chief priests

---

[1] Pontus Pilate was the Roman Governor of Judea that ruled from 26 A.D. to 36 A.D. (Burge, *John*, 498).

[2] The Jews desired Jesus to be crucified but needed to operate within the Roman court system to achieve what they desired. Under roman control, only the roman officials had the power to give capital punishment (MacArthur, *The MacArthur Bible Commentary*, 1417).

[3] Flogging was a beating using a whip with leather wrapped pieces of bone or metal (Carson, *John*, 597). The beating was so savage that the victims sometimes died (Ibid.).

[4] The mocking of Jesus continues with the crown thorns piercing his skull and the purple robe, designated for royalty attempting to humiliate Jesus.

and the officers saw him, they cried out, "Crucify him, crucify him!" Pilate said to them, "Take him yourselves and crucify him, for I find no guilt in him." [7] The Jews answered him, "We have a law, and according to that law he ought to die because he has made himself the Son of God." [8] When Pilate heard this statement, he was even more afraid. [9] He entered his headquarters again and said to Jesus, "Where are you from?" But Jesus gave him no answer. [10] So Pilate said to him, "You will not speak to me? Do you not know that I have authority to release you and authority to crucify you?" [11] Jesus answered him, "You would have no authority over me at all unless it had been given you from above. Therefore he who delivered me over to you has the greater sin."

[12] From then on Pilate sought to release him, but the Jews cried out, "If you release this man, you are not Caesar's friend. Everyone who makes himself a king opposes Caesar." [13] So when Pilate heard these words, he brought Jesus out and sat down on the judgment seat at a place called The Stone Pavement, and in Aramaic Gabbatha. [14] Now it was the day of Preparation of the Passover. It was about the sixth hour. He said to the Jews, "Behold your King!" [15] They cried out, "Away with him, away with him, crucify him!" Pilate said to them, "Shall I crucify your King?" The chief priests answered, "We have no king but Caesar."[5] [16] So he delivered him over to them to be crucified.

So they took Jesus, [17] and he went out, bearing his own cross, to the place called The Place of a Skull, which in Aramaic is called Golgotha. [18] There they crucified him, and with him two others, one on either side, and Jesus between them. [19] Pilate also wrote an inscription and put it on the cross. It read, "Jesus of Nazareth, the King of the Jews." [20] Many of the Jews read this inscription, for the place where Jesus was crucified was near the city, and it was written in Aramaic, in Latin, and in Greek.

One Big Thing:

One Confusing Thing:

---

[5] The king of Israel ought to have been God but as Israel did in 1 Samuel, God's kingship has been rejected. Now, the Jews have abandoned God's sent one and wed themselves to Caesar.

What role does Pilate play in the Jewish plot to kill Jesus?

How does Pilate's view of Jesus change throughout this conversation?

Jesus states in 18:36: "My kingdom is not of this world." What does he mean? What is the purpose of Jesus' kingdom?

Why didn't Jesus defend himself?

If Jesus didn't defend himself, should we?

What aspects of Pilate's character are revealed through this conversation? Do you see any of these in yourself?

What are the implications of the Jews saying "We have no king but Caesar"? Who should be the king of Israel?

Why does Jesus seemingly conceal himself throughout the Gospels?

One Way I Must Respond

Who is Jesus to Pilate?

Scriptures to consider:
Matthew 26:39
Romans 13:1
Philippians 2:5-11
Matthew 5:38-41

Thomas

LESSON 11

Thomas
John 20:18-29

For context, this is after Jesus' death and resurrection.

[18] Mary Magdalene[1] went and announced to the disciples, "I have seen the Lord"— and that he had said these things to her.

[19] On the evening of that day, the first day of the week, the doors being locked[2] where the disciples were for fear of the Jews, Jesus came and stood among them and said to them, "Peace be with you."[3] [20] When he had said this, he showed them his hands and his side. Then the disciples were glad when they saw the Lord. [21] Jesus said to them again, "Peace be with you. As the Father has sent me, even so I am sending you." [22] And when he had said this, he breathed on them and said to them, "Receive the Holy Spirit. [23] If you forgive the sins of any, they are forgiven them; if you withhold forgiveness from any, it is withheld."[4]

[24] Now Thomas, one of the twelve, called the Twin, was not with them when Jesus came. [25] So the other disciples told him, "We have seen the Lord." But he said to them, "Unless I see in his hands the mark of the nails, and place my finger into the mark of the nails, and place my hand into his side, I will never believe."

[26] Eight days later,[5] his disciples were inside again, and Thomas was with them. Although the doors were locked, Jesus came and stood among them and said, "Peace be with you." [27] Then he said to Thomas, "Put your finger here, and see my hands; and put out your hand, and place it in my side. Do not disbelieve, but believe." [28] Thomas answered him, "My Lord and my God!"[6] [29] Jesus said to him, "Have you believed because you have seen me? Blessed are those who have not seen and yet have believed."[7]

---

[1] Mary Magdalene is a devout follower of Jesus. She once was possessed by seven demons (Luke 8:2) but after her healing she has spent her life following Jesus. Mary is standing at the foot of the cross as Jesus dies and is the first to approach the tomb on Resurrection Sunday.

[2] After observing the death of Jesus, the disciples feared a similar fate at the hands of the Jews (MacArthur, *The MacArthur Bible Commentary*, 1424)

[3] Jesus' greeting of "Peace be with you" connects to his final words "It is finished". Reconciliation (peace) between God and man has been accomplished (Carson, *John*, 647).

[4] Jesus is not saying Christians now have the power to forgive sins. Instead, Christians are able to boldly declare that sins can and have been forgive for all who believe (MacArthur, *The MacArthur Bible Commentary*, 1424).

[5] There is silence from Jesus for eight days. How long must this have felt for not only Thomas but for all of the disciples.

[6] Thomas is not only affirming the resurrection, but also affirming the identity of Jesus as the Messiah of God (Carson, *John*, 659). This is a heartfelt belief in Jesus (Burge, *John*, 563)). "This must be the anthem of every believer that follows Jesus (Carson, *John*, 659).

[7] See 1 Peter 1:8

One Big Thing:

One Confusing Thing:

Was Thomas wrong to want proof?

How do we balance our desire for proof while maintaining faith?

How would you explain the idea of faith to a skeptic?

Return to lesson 1 question 4 on doubts. Has your answer to this question developed over the course of this study?

What is the full meaning of Thomas' confession: "my Lord and my God"?

How can you live out this confession?

How has God revealed himself to you?

How has your view of Jesus changed throughout the study of *Conversations with Jesus*?

One Way I Must Respond

Who is Jesus to Thomas?

Scriptures to Consider:
1 Peter 1:8
Hebrews 11:1
John 14:5-7
Romans 5:1-2

Bibliography

Blomberg, Craig. Matthew (New American Commentary Series). Nashville: Broadman Press, 1992.

Burge, Gary M. John (The NIV Application Commentary Series). Grand Rapids: Zondervan Publishing House, 2000.

Carson, D.A. The Gospel According to John (The Pillar New Testament Commentary Series). Grand Rapids: William B. Eerdsman Publishing Company, 1991.

Kistemaker, Simon. The Conversations of Jesus. Grand Rapids: Baker Books, 2004.

Lane, William L. The Gospel of Mark (The New International Commentary on the New Testament). Grand Rapids: William B. Eerdsman Publishing Company, 1974.

MacArthur, John. *The MacArthur Bible Commentary* (Nashville: Thomas Nelson, 2005).

Stein, Robert H. John (New American Commentary Series). Nashville: Broadman Press, 1992.

Wilkins, Michael J. Matthew (The NIV Application Commentary Series). Grand Rapids: Zondervan Publishing House, 2004.

Made in the USA
Middletown, DE
31 July 2020